Rolling Along

Rolling Along

Out for a Ride

Out for a Ride

Another Tough TONKA Truck

Another Tough TONKA Truck!

A Heavy Load

TONKA covers some rough terrain!

Built to Last

TONKA saves the day!

TONKA saves the day!

TONKA vehicles are always ready for action!

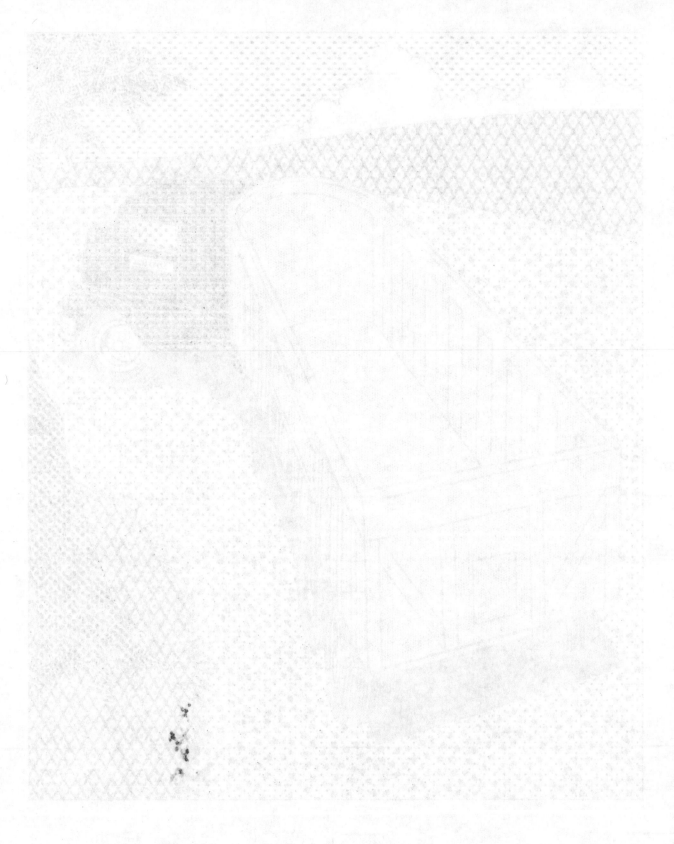

Heading Home

Tough Enough

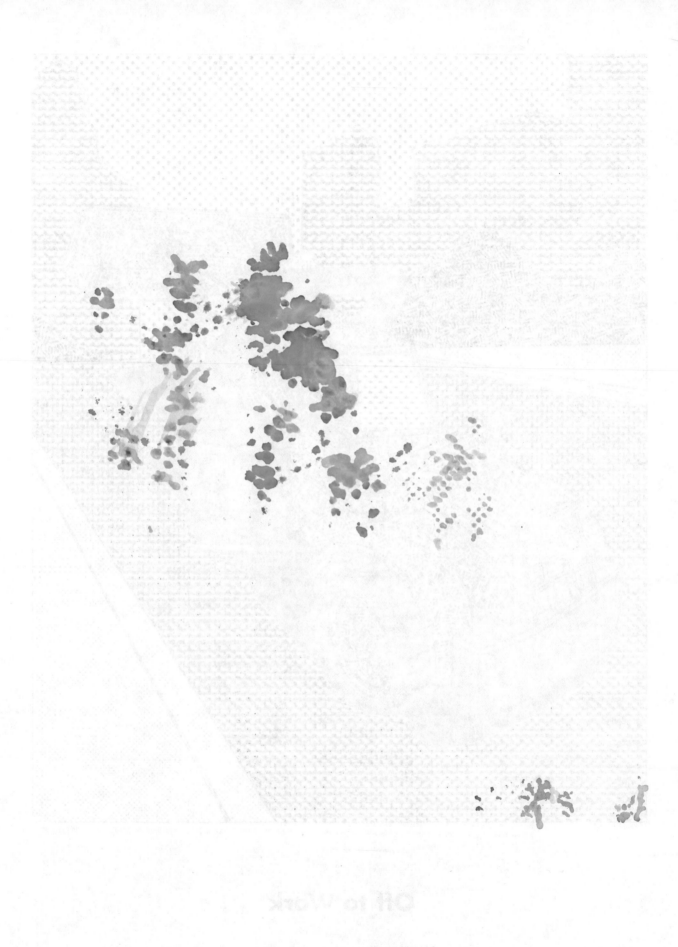

Off to Work